My Sermon Notes

_____

_____

_____

_____

Some of my Favorite Scripture Readings & Verses

Today's Sermon Notes

Date:

Speaker:

Scripture:

Notes:

Themes & Key Points:

Personal Reflections & Main Takeaways:

Questions or Ideas to Explore Further:

Today's Sermon Notes

Date:

Speaker:

Scripture:

Notes:

Themes & Key Points:

Personal Reflections & Main Takeaways:

Questions or Ideas to Explore Further:

Today's Sermon Notes

Date:

Speaker:

Scripture:

Notes:

Themes & Key Points:

Personal Reflections & Main Takeaways:

Questions or Ideas to Explore Further:

Today's Sermon Notes

Date:

Speaker:

Scripture:

Notes:

Themes & Key Points:

Personal Reflections & Main Takeaways:

Questions or Ideas to Explore Further:

Today's Sermon Notes

Date:

Speaker:

Scripture:

Notes:

Themes & Key Points:

Personal Reflections & Main Takeaways:

Questions or Ideas to Explore Further:

Today's Sermon Notes

Date:

Speaker:

Scripture:

Notes:

Themes & Key Points:

Personal Reflections & Main Takeaways:

Questions or Ideas to Explore Further:

Today's Sermon Notes

Date:

Speaker:

Scripture:

Notes:

Themes & Key Points:

Personal Reflections & Main Takeaways:

Questions or Ideas to Explore Further:

Today's Sermon Notes

Date:

Speaker:

Scripture:

Notes:

Themes & Key Points:

Personal Reflections & Main Takeaways:

Questions or Ideas to Explore Further:

Today's Sermon Notes

Date:

Speaker:

Scripture:

Notes:

Themes & Key Points:

Personal Reflections & Main Takeaways:

Questions or Ideas to Explore Further:

Today's Sermon Notes

Date:

Speaker:

Scripture:

Notes:

Themes & Key Points:

Personal Reflections & Main Takeaways:

Questions or Ideas to Explore Further:

Today's Sermon Notes

Date:

Speaker:

Scripture:

Notes:

Themes & Key Points:

Personal Reflections & Main Takeaways:

Questions or Ideas to Explore Further:

Today's Sermon Notes

Date:

Speaker:

Scripture:

Notes:

Themes & Key Points:

Personal Reflections & Main Takeaways:

Questions or Ideas to Explore Further:

Today's Sermon Notes

Date:

Speaker:

Scripture:

Notes:

Themes & Key Points:

Personal Reflections & Main Takeaways:

Questions or Ideas to Explore Further:

Today's Sermon Notes

Date:

Speaker:

Scripture:

Notes:

Themes & Key Points:

Personal Reflections & Main Takeaways:

Questions or Ideas to Explore Further:

Today's Sermon Notes

Date:

Speaker:

Scripture:

Notes:

Themes & Key Points:

Personal Reflections & Main Takeaways:

Questions or Ideas to Explore Further:

Today's Sermon Notes

Date:

Speaker:

Scripture:

Notes:

Themes & Key Points:

Personal Reflections & Main Takeaways:

Questions or Ideas to Explore Further:

Today's Sermon Notes

Date:	
Speaker:	

Scripture:

Notes:

Themes & Key Points:

Personal Reflections & Main Takeaways:

Questions or Ideas to Explore Further:

Today's Sermon Notes

Date:

Speaker:

Scripture:

Notes:

Themes & Key Points:

Personal Reflections & Main Takeaways:

Questions or Ideas to Explore Further:

Today's Sermon Notes

Date:	
Speaker:	

Scripture:

Notes:

Themes & Key Points:

Personal Reflections & Main Takeaways:

Questions or Ideas to Explore Further:

Today's Sermon Notes

Date:

Speaker:

Scripture:

Notes:

Themes & Key Points:

Personal Reflections & Main Takeaways:

Questions or Ideas to Explore Further:

Today's Sermon Notes

Date:

Speaker:

Scripture:

Notes:

Themes & Key Points:

Personal Reflections & Main Takeaways:

Questions or Ideas to Explore Further:

Today's Sermon Notes

Date:

Speaker:

Scripture:

Notes:

Themes & Key Points:

Personal Reflections & Main Takeaways:

Questions or Ideas to Explore Further:

Today's Sermon Notes

Date:
Speaker:

Scripture:

Notes:

Themes & Key Points:

Personal Reflections & Main Takeaways:

Questions or Ideas to Explore Further:

Today's Sermon Notes

Date:

Speaker:

Scripture:

Notes:

Themes & Key Points:

Personal Reflections & Main Takeaways:

Questions or Ideas to Explore Further:

Today's Sermon Notes

Date:

Speaker:

Scripture:

Notes:

Themes & Key Points:

Personal Reflections & Main Takeaways:

Questions or Ideas to Explore Further:

Today's Sermon Notes

Date:

Speaker:

Scripture:

Notes:

Themes & Key Points:

Personal Reflections & Main Takeaways:

Questions or Ideas to Explore Further:

Today's Sermon Notes

Date:

Speaker:

Scripture:

Notes:

Themes & Key Points:

Personal Reflections & Main Takeaways:

Questions or Ideas to Explore Further:

Today's Sermon Notes

Date:

Speaker:

Scripture:

Notes:

Themes & Key Points:

Personal Reflections & Main Takeaways:

Questions or Ideas to Explore Further:

Today's Sermon Notes

| Date: |
| Speaker: |

Scripture:

Notes:

Themes & Key Points:

Personal Reflections & Main Takeaways:

Questions or Ideas to Explore Further:

Today's Sermon Notes

Date:

Speaker:

Scripture:

Notes:

Themes & Key Points:

Personal Reflections & Main Takeaways:

Questions or Ideas to Explore Further:

Today's Sermon Notes

Date:

Speaker:

Scripture:

Notes:

Themes & Key Points:

Personal Reflections & Main Takeaways:

Questions or Ideas to Explore Further:

Today's Sermon Notes

Date:

Speaker:

Scripture:

Notes:

Themes & Key Points:

Personal Reflections & Main Takeaways:

Questions or Ideas to Explore Further:

Today's Sermon Notes

Date:
Speaker:

Scripture:

Notes:

Themes & Key Points:

Personal Reflections & Main Takeaways:

Questions or Ideas to Explore Further:

Today's Sermon Notes

Date:

Speaker:

Scripture:

Notes:

Themes & Key Points:

Personal Reflections & Main Takeaways:

Questions or Ideas to Explore Further:

Today's Sermon Notes

Date:

Speaker:

Scripture:

Notes:

Themes & Key Points:

Personal Reflections & Main Takeaways:

Questions or Ideas to Explore Further:

Today's Sermon Notes

Date:

Speaker:

Scripture:

Notes:

Themes & Key Points:

Personal Reflections & Main Takeaways:

Questions or Ideas to Explore Further:

Today's Sermon Notes

Date:

Speaker:

Scripture:

Notes:

Themes & Key Points:

Personal Reflections & Main Takeaways:

Questions or Ideas to Explore Further:

Today's Sermon Notes

Date:

Speaker:

Scripture:

Notes:

Themes & Key Points:

Personal Reflections & Main Takeaways:

Questions or Ideas to Explore Further:

Today's Sermon Notes

Date:

Speaker:

Scripture:

Notes:

Themes & Key Points:

Personal Reflections & Main Takeaways:

Questions or Ideas to Explore Further:

Today's Sermon Notes

Date:

Speaker:

Scripture:

Notes:

Themes & Key Points:

Personal Reflections & Main Takeaways:

Questions or Ideas to Explore Further:

Today's Sermon Notes

Date:
Speaker:

Scripture:

Notes:

Themes & Key Points:

Personal Reflections & Main Takeaways:

Questions or Ideas to Explore Further:

Today's Sermon Notes

Date:

Speaker:

Scripture:

Notes:

Themes & Key Points:

Personal Reflections & Main Takeaways:

Questions or Ideas to Explore Further:

Today's Sermon Notes

Date:

Speaker:

Scripture:

Notes:

Themes & Key Points:

Personal Reflections & Main Takeaways:

Questions or Ideas to Explore Further:

Today's Sermon Notes

Date:

Speaker:

Scripture:

Notes:

Themes & Key Points:

Personal Reflections & Main Takeaways:

Questions or Ideas to Explore Further:

Today's Sermon Notes

Date:

Speaker:

Scripture:

Notes:

Themes & Key Points:

Personal Reflections & Main Takeaways:

Questions or Ideas to Explore Further:

Today's Sermon Notes

Date:

Speaker:

Scripture:

Notes:

Themes & Key Points:

Personal Reflections & Main Takeaways:

Questions or Ideas to Explore Further:

Today's Sermon Notes

Date:

Speaker:

Scripture:

Notes:

Themes & Key Points:

Personal Reflections & Main Takeaways:

Questions or Ideas to Explore Further:

Today's Sermon Notes

Date:

Speaker:

Scripture:

Notes:

Today's Sermon Notes

Date:	
Speaker:	

Scripture:

Notes:

Themes & Key Points:

Personal Reflections & Main Takeaways:

Questions or Ideas to Explore Further:

Themes & Key Points:

Personal Reflections & Main Takeaways:

Questions or Ideas to Explore Further:

Today's Sermon Notes

Date:

Speaker:

Scripture:

Notes:

Themes & Key Points:

Personal Reflections & Main Takeaways:

Questions or Ideas to Explore Further:

Today's Sermon Notes

Date:	
Speaker:	

Scripture:

Notes:

Themes & Key Points:

Personal Reflections & Main Takeaways:

Questions or Ideas to Explore Further:

Today's Sermon Notes

Date:

Speaker:

Scripture:

Notes:

Themes & Key Points:

Personal Reflections & Main Takeaways:

Questions or Ideas to Explore Further:

Today's Sermon Notes

Date:

Speaker:

Scripture:

Notes:

Themes & Key Points:

Personal Reflections & Main Takeaways:

Questions or Ideas to Explore Further:

Today's Sermon Notes

Date:	
Speaker:	

Scripture:

Notes:

Themes & Key Points:

Personal Reflections & Main Takeaways:

Questions or Ideas to Explore Further:

Today's Sermon Notes

Date:

Speaker:

Scripture:

Notes:

Themes & Key Points:

Personal Reflections & Main Takeaways:

Questions or Ideas to Explore Further:

Today's Sermon Notes

Date:

Speaker:

Scripture:

Notes:

Themes & Key Points:

Personal Reflections & Main Takeaways:

Questions or Ideas to Explore Further:

Today's Sermon Notes

| Date: | |
| Speaker: | |

Scripture:

Notes:

Themes & Key Points:

Personal Reflections & Main Takeaways:

Questions or Ideas to Explore Further:

Today's Sermon Notes

Date:

Speaker:

Scripture:

Notes:

Themes & Key Points:

Personal Reflections & Main Takeaways:

Questions or Ideas to Explore Further:

Made in the USA
Monee, IL
31 March 2021